THE OFFICIAL **RSPCA** PET GUIDE

Care for Your

HarperCollins*Publishers*

First published in 1980 by
William Collins Sons & Co Ltd, London
New edition published in 1990

Reprinted by
HarperCollins*Publishers*
77-85 Fulham Palace Road
Hammersmith
London W6 8JB

The HarperCollins website address is
www.**fire**and**water**.com

07 06 05 04 03 02 01
16 15 14 13 12 11 10

This is a fully revised and extended edition of *Care for your Cat*, first
published in 1980 and reprinted 10 times, with revisions in 1985

Text of the 1980 edition by Tina Hearne; text revisions and additions for
this edition by Angela Rixon Sayer

Designed and edited by The Templar Company plc
Pippbrook Mill, London Road, Dorking, Surrey RH4 1JE

Front cover photograph: Animal Ark, London
Text photographs: Animal Photography Ltd, John Clegg,
Bruce Coleman Ltd, Marc Henrie, Solitaire *(also back cover, centre
and bottom)*, Tony Stone Worldwide, Syndication International,
The Wellcome Foundation, ZEFA

Illustrations: George Thompson, Carole Lawson and
Fred Anderson/Bernard Thornton Artists

**A catalogue record for this book is available
from the British Library**

ISBN 0 00 412542 8

Printed by Midas Printing Ltd, Hong Kong

First things first, animals are fun. Anybody who has ever enjoyed the company of a pet knows well enough just how strong the bond between human and animal can be. Elderly or lonely people often depend on a pet for their only company, and this can be a rewarding relationship for both human and animal. Doctors have proved that animals can be instrumental in the prevention of and recovery from mental or physical disease. Children learn the meaning of loyalty, unselfishness and friendship by growing up with animals.

But the commitment to an animal doesn't begin and end with a visit to the local pet shop. A pet should never be given as a 'surprise' present. The decision to bring a pet into your home should always be discussed and agreed by all the members of your family. Bear in mind that parents are ultimately responsible for the health and well-being of the animal for the whole of its lifetime. If you are not prepared for the inevitable expense, time, patience and occasional frustration involved, then the RSPCA would much rather that you didn't have a pet.

Armed with the facts, aware of the pitfalls but still confident of your ability to give a pet a good home, the next step is to find where you can get an animal from. Seek the advice of a veterinary surgeon or RSPCA Inspector about reputable local breeders or suppliers. Do consider the possibility of offering a home to an animal from an RSPCA establishment. There are no animals more deserving of loving owners.

As for the care of your pet, you should find in this book all you need to know to keep it happy, healthy and rewarding for many years to come. Responsible ownership means happy pets. Enjoy the experience!

Terence C. Bate

Terence Bate BVSc, LLB, MRCVS
Chief Veterinary Officer, RSPCA

Introduction

Cats were first domesticated about four thousand years ago, by the Egyptians, and it is known from ancient works of art that the Abyssinian, with its agouti coat, although a modern breed, most resembles the cats of Ancient Egypt.

Cats were not domesticated in Europe before Roman times. In Europe, the Tabbies are thought to have been early mutations, and tabby markings still show on kittens of many later breeds descended from them.

Today there are about a hundred varieties of pedigree cat to choose from, but by far the greatest number of household cats are mongrel. The breeding propensity of the cat, together with its independent lifestyle, makes certain a very high percentage of mongrel kittens.

Cats are perhaps the easiest household pets, and yet because they are independent, mostly undemanding, largely self sufficient and good survivors, some owners tend to be more casual and irresponsible about them than any other animal.

The cat is not a good choice of pet for people who are out all day; nor is it a good choice for a family living in a house where the cat has easy access to a busy road; nor is it responsible to allow cats to mix with others without first having been neutered.

Cats are generally easy to care for and undemanding, but their reputation for independence does not mean they can be neglected. Given a good home they will provide years of rewarding companionship.

Pedigree or mongrel?

MONGREL CATS

Most household cats are mongrel, and very often adopted into the family on impulse. Such easily acquired cats may not have been inoculated against the infectious cat diseases, or have been wormed. They should be taken for veterinary examination, and neutered. It should be understood that although they may cost nothing at all to adopt, once taken into the household they will cost just as much as any other cat.

There is no reason, however, why they should not make delightful companions. Many are beautiful; all are graceful; most are affectionate and easy to care for. Their hardiness depends very largely on their background. In general, mongrels are stronger than highly bred animals of the same species but if, as often happens with cats, the mongrels are the product of a mating between immature parents, then they and their kittens are likely to be undersized and frailer than most.

Mongrel cats are often hardier and just as appealing as pedigrees.

PEDIGREE CATS

Pedigree cats are usually acquired deliberately, rather than accidentally, and tend to be more carefully supervised than most mongrels. They are perhaps more prone to suffer from over-feeding and lack of exercise.

Their character is a most pertinent consideration. The Foreign and Oriental breeds, and in particular the Siamese, are untypical of cats in their loyalty to a person, from whom they demand a great deal of attention in the most vocal way. Some are notorious for being noisy cats, especially the females when calling, but their undoubted grace and intelligence outweighs this disadvantage for most people. Orientals are also unusual in that they will allow themselves to be exercised on a lead.

Long-haired cats, whether pedigree or mongrel, are demanding in that they should be groomed at least once a day, and devotees of long-haired breeds groom two or three times a day.

Male or female

If pet cats are neutered there is little to choose between the sexes – either make excellent pets.

An entire male, or tom cat, is really regarded as unsuitable for most households, for he will spend most of his days searching out female cats on heat, returning home only for sleep and for food. Although a tom may have a very pleasing and loving disposition towards people, he will frequently spray his pungent urine in the house to mark out his territory. Some tom cats will also leave piles of uncovered faeces in the house too, as territory markers. Because toms spend so much time away from home, they inevitably become involved in fights with neighbouring toms over territory, or the possession of a female. Such cats soon develop a disagreeable tom-cat smell. The bites and scratches sustained during their scuffles usually become infected, and may result in the formation of large abscesses, needing veterinary treatment.

Unspayed females, or queens, are considered more suitable as pets, but they are difficult to contain when in season, very tiresome when they call, and likely to produce many litters in their lifetime.

For these reasons the RSPCA recommends that all household cats be neutered.

British Black, showing characteristic heavy jowls of an older tom cat, and the delicate features of an Abyssinian queen.

Female

Male

The distance between the anus and the urinary tract opening is very short and inclined to be slit-shaped in females; in males the distance is rather longer and the aperture more rounded.

Neutering

Why should I have my cat neutered?

The unsocial habits of an unneutered tom are described on the previous page. A female cat will come into season about every two to three weeks for around eight months of the year. As time goes on, it will become increasingly difficult to prevent her from becoming pregnant – and just as difficult to find a first-class home for every kitten (a cat can have three pregnancies a year and may have up to five or six kittens in each litter). Many thousands of unwanted kittens are destroyed each year and the least we can do is not to add to their number.

What does the neutering operation consist of?

In the female cat 'spaying' consists of removing the womb and ovaries in an operation known as an ovaro-hysterectomy. In the male, the testicles are removed in an operation known as castration. Spaying and castration are carried out under general anaesthesia, so the cat feels no pain. Recovery is rapid.

Should I let my cat have one litter first?

It is a popular myth that cats and dogs 'ought' to be allowed at least one litter. There is no good reason for letting your cat have a litter before being spayed.

Will neutering change my cat's personality or make it fat?

In the female there is virtually no change in personality at all. In the male, the change is only for the better – he will not wander or spray the house; he will not smell and he will not be aggressive to other cats.

Neutered cats only become fat if overfed (see p.27). Some neutered cats display symptoms caused by slight disturbances in their hormone levels. Any form of skin condition like eczema may be suspected as hormonal in origin, and veterinary advice should be sought, so that any imbalance can be treated.

Can the neutering operation be carried out on an older cat?

Ideally, a tom should be castrated between five and six months old, and a queen spayed at about the same age, but neutering can be carried out at virtually any age, provided the cat is fit and healthy.

Breed varieties

LONGHAIR CATS

The first long-haired cats were brought to Europe in the sixteenth century, and were called Angoras, after the city of that name (now Ankara, capital of modern Turkey, from where they are believed to have originated). Other long-coated cats were brought from Persia and from these two types are descended the modern breed Persians or Longhairs.

The **Persian** has a round broad head, stubby nose, large round eyes, and tiny tufted ears. Its body is chunky, and its thick short legs have large round paws. Each variety is named after its coat colour, so a white-coated cat is known as the White Persian or Longhaired White, and so on. There is a very wide range of permitted colours and patterns.

The original **Turkish Angora** still exists as a separate breed and is also found in a wide range of colours. It has a silkier coat than the Persian and a lithe, more graceful body. It is comparatively little known. Another cat native to Turkey is an oddity: the **Turkish Van**, named after Lake Van, enjoys swimming and playing with water. It is always white with patches of either auburn or cream on the head and tail.

Other long-haired breeds are more like the Angoras than the Persians in shape, having longer noses, larger ears, longer, finer bodies and less fullness to the coat. There are also Longhairs which are variations on short-haired breeds: the **Balinese** is the long-coated version of the popular Siamese, while the **Somali** is a long-haired Abyssinian and the **Cymric** a long-haired Manx. The **Birman** has 'Siamese' colouring except for the lower legs and paws which are pure white.

There are also long-haired varieties which come from North America – among them the large **Maine Coon** and the **Ragdoll**, which gets its name from its curious habit of going completely limp when picked up.

Before committing yourself to a long-haired cat, remember that it will need regular daily grooming.

Bi-colour Persian

Chinchilla Persian

Balinese

SHORTHAIR CATS

The **British Shorthair**, like the Persian, is stocky, with a broad round head, large round eyes, small round ears and a short thick tail. There is also the **Exotic Shorthair**, the true short-coated version of the Persian, being bred from Persian and British Shorthair parentage.

British Blue Shorthair

The Isle of Man is not unique in being the home to a breed of tailless cat, but the **Manx** has a long tradition and was considered a lucky symbol. Another cat in which natural mutation has produced a physical anomaly is the **Scottish Fold**, distinguished by its folded ears.

Other short-haired breeds have a quite different body configuration from the British and Exotic Shorthairs. These are described collectively as Foreign Shorthairs.

Cats of the Foreign group tend to be slim and lithe, with long faces, large ears, long slim legs and long pointed tails. The **Abyssinian** is said to resemble the cats revered in Ancient Egypt and has, unique among cats, a 'ticked' coat. The **Russian Blue** has a distinctive dense coat, dark slate grey in colour, and green eyes, while the similarly coloured **Korat**, from Thailand, has a smooth coat and a heart-shaped face. **Burmese** cats are slightly stockier and are renowned for their intelligence and good nature.

Mackerel Striped Tabby

Other Foreign Shorthairs include the shiny black **Bombay**, **Burmillas** and the distinctive Rexes.

There are two main breeds of curly-coated **Rex** cats, named after the English counties in which they were first discovered: the Cornish Rex and the Devon Rex. The Cornish has the more luxurious coat, and is quite Oriental in configuration, while the Devon, with its softly waved coat, has a rather pixie-like look.

ORIENTALS

Siamese and the varieties derived from them are known as Oriental cats. All are slim with wedge-shaped heads, large pointed ears, long slim legs and tiny oval paws. They are inquisitive and intelligent. The Siamese have colour only on the 'points' of mask (face), ears, legs, paws and tail. They are named after the colour of the points. The seal-brown is known as the Seal Point Siamese, and so on. All Siamese cats (and one of the derived breeds, the **Oriental** or **Foreign White**), have brilliant blue eyes. All the other Oriental Shorthairs have bright green eyes and, having lost the gene which restricts the coat colour to the points, are evenly coloured all over.

Cornish Rex

Seal Point Siamese

Biology

Backbone The combination of an extremely supple backbone and powerful back muscles gives the cat a great range of movement, including the ability to arch its back in this way. It also allows a falling cat to twist in mid-air to right its position for a correct landing.

Tail The magnificent tail of the cat has many biological uses. It is a muffler against the cold; a balance in climbing and jumping; a protection against flies; a communications signal; and both a warning and a distraction to an enemy.

The curious tailless Manx cat has not fallen victim to the practice of tail-docking. It is a mutant form of cat with only three tail vertebrae. Other cats may have as many as twenty-four.

Tailless Manx cat

Characteristic arching of back

Claws for attack and defence

Claws A cat's claws are of the greatest importance to the animal, being a weapon of both attack and defence, and an aid to climbing. Cats take care to keep their claws in good trim, sharpening them on a scratching post by pulling off the damaged outer layer of claw to expose a new layer beneath. When not in use, all but the dew claws are retracted into a protective sheath that saves them from becoming blunted.

Whiskers The whiskers, or vibrissae, are modified hairs which serve as tactile organs. Whiskers are extremely sensitive to touch, since they grow from hair follicles that are abundantly well supplied with nerve-endings.

It is also thought that the whiskers allow a cat to judge the width of an opening, since the extent of the whiskers, from tip to tip, is equivalent to the maximum width of the body.

Tongue The surface of the cat's tongue is covered with small projections, or papillae, that account for its characteristic roughness. This surface makes the tongue a very effective tool for feeding, particularly for rasping flesh from bones, and an equally effective tool for grooming.

An effective grooming aid

Ears It often happens that a blue-eyed white cat is deaf. Nevertheless, most cats have a highly developed sense of hearing. They are able to move the external ears, the pinnae, in the direction of sound, so that the sound waves are collected and conducted down to the ear-drum for transmission to the inner ear.

The pinnae also allow the cat to judge the distance and direction of sound. The sound from a particular source is heard fractionally differently in each ear, and from this the cat is able to estimate the source of sound very accurately. It has been demonstrated that a cat can distinguish between the sources of two adjacent sounds, 18 metres/ 20 yards away, that are only half a metre/18 in from each other.

The inner ear is also the organ of balance. When its fluid-filled cavities and canals are stimulated by tilting and rotating movements, reflex actions are triggered that return the body to its normal position. This function of the ear is of paramount importance to an agile, arboreal animal like the cat, and because of it the cat is reputed always to land on its feet.

The teeth of a carnivore

Teeth Being a naturally short-faced animal, the cat has a set of only 30 teeth, whereas a dog has 42. An adult cat has 12 incisors, 4 canines, 10 premolars and 4 molars.

The cat's teeth are those of the true carnivore, perfectly adapted for the diet of a meat-eater. The prominent canines, or fangs, are used to kill prey, and to tear meat from a carcass. The molars, or cheek teeth, have blade-like edges for slicing flesh into pieces small enough to swallow.

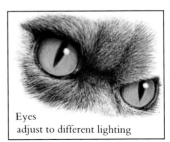

Eyes
adjust to different lighting

Eyes The cat hunts more by sight than smell, aided by extremely efficient eyesight that adjusts instanteously to changing lighting conditions. In bright light the pupil will contract to a mere longitudinal slit; in poor light it will dilate to take advantage of the faintest gleam.

In very bad light the cat's eyes appear to shine, giving rise to the claim that cats can see in the dark. This is not so, but in poor lighting the eyes, like the road studs named after them, are able to reflect back any available light so that they appear to glow.

Selecting a cat

Once you have decided to share your life with a cat, you have to make up your mind whether you would prefer a pedigree or a mongrel, a male or a female, an adult cat or a kitten.

Kittens are endearing and full of fun, enchanting to watch at play – and few people can resist them. However, they do need house training, feeding up to five times a day to begin with, and can often prove very time-consuming for the first few months. They will also enthusiastically claw curtains and chair legs, and where there are very young children or elderly people about, they are in danger of being trodden underfoot or causing an accident. Although they soon grow from playful balls of destruction into amiable and often perfect pets, for these reasons many people prefer to consider taking on an adult cat rather than a young kitten.

If you do not want the problems connected with the acquisition of a young kitten, you could approach your local RSPCA branch to see if there are any pet cats in need of homes. If you are away from home for most of the day you might decide to get two cats, so that they are company for one another. Rather than acquiring a cat on impulse, make up your mind exactly what you would like, then set about finding the right pet for you.

Before you get a cat or a kitten it is worth while asking yourself a few basic questions.

Pet owners moving abroad or into accommodation unsuitable for cats will always be grateful to find a good home for their pet.

- Do you have a garden or safe access to the great outdoors?
- Are you home for at least part of the day, every day?
- Are you willing to put up with the possible damage that claws can do to furnishings?
- Are you willing to bear the cost of vaccinations and possible veterinary attention? (Pet insurance can help cover some of these costs.) All but those cats kept specifically for breeding should be neutered at about six months of age, and all kittens and young cats should be

Pedigree cats like this Birman Sealpoint can be expensive to buy, but they come with the reassurance of a reliable source and a documented background.

vaccinated against feline infectious enteritis and feline influenza, which require booster vaccinations throughout their lifetime.
- Are you willing to pay for boarding your cat when you go on holiday, or have you caring neighbours who would feed and look after it for you?

If you cannot honestly answer 'yes' to all these questions, please think very carefully before you get a cat or kitten.

SOURCES

Ask friends, neighbours, local vets, and check local newspaper advertisements rather than pet shops; the regional RSPCA or cat rescue office may also be able to help. Many people cannot keep their pets for a variety of reasons and are happy to find a good home for their adult cat. Enquire about vaccinations and find out as much as you can about the cat's background – knowing its habits and fears will help you to settle it in and make it feel at home.

A cat might 'adopt' you, turning up daily on the doorstep, but beware you are not inadvertently enticing a cat away from its home with your attentions.

If you want to find out more about pedigree cats, first read up about them in an up-to-date reference book. Visit a cat show where you will be able to see many types of pedigree cats, and where you can meet and talk with owners and breeders.

Choose a cat that will suit you and your lifestyle. Cats do vary greatly, and it is vital that you have the time to care for your pet and that you are both of the same basic temperament.

Housing

Hooded litter tray

CAT BED

The only accommodation a cat really needs in the house is a good bed, which may be any comfortable chair, box, or basket, but should not be one of the household's beds or chairs. Fleas sometimes cling to even the best kept cats, and would lay their eggs in the bedding or upholstery.

A variety of manufactured cat beds is available, made of such materials as fibreglass, rigid plastic, canvas or basket-work. They should be raised off the ground, clear of draughts and dampness, and when a bed has no legs as in our illustration, the base must be slightly domed to leave air space underneath.

A washable cushion or blanket will keep the cat comfortable, and providing he always has access to his bed, heating is unnecessary, except rarely for old or sick cats, or for very young kittens in severe weather conditions.

Cat bed

LITTER TRAY

Cats are the most fastidious of animals, and from a very early age will scratch out a hole before they defecate, and then cover over the traces with earth. This has a natural survival value in the wild, since it serves to hide the presence of the nest of young kittens, and in captivity makes the cat one of the cleanest pets.

Cats are easily house trained to urinate and defecate in a tray filled with dry earth, sand, or a proprietary cat litter sprinkled with earth. It is important to use some earth, or the cat may fail to make the transition to defecating in the garden. The tray will need to be kept scrupulously clean, and in a dark secluded position where the cat will feel it is private enough to use.

Scratching post

Hooded litter trays are ideal for cats which prefer their toilet arrangements to be private. The hood lifts off for ease of cleaning and the extra deep base prevents litter from being scratched out on to the floor.

City cats, with no safe access to a garden, may need to use a tray for life, and many adult cats need one at night.

SCRATCHING POST

The cat uses its claws in climbing, in defence, and in attack, and has to keep them in immaculate condition if they are to serve these purposes. They are normally held sheathed, to protect them from being blunted in wear.

Many cats will sharpen their claws on a tree trunk in the garden; others select a particular item of furniture or upholstery in the house, and may damage it severely with constant use.

In an attempt to forestall such damage, some owners provide a scratching post. Any good-sized length of log with its bark on will be suitable, or a piece of sacking or heavy upholstery material nailed to a board makes a satisfactory decoy from the armchairs.

At pet accessory stores, a whole range of manufactured scratching posts is available. These include a bark-covered post impregnated with catnip; another, covered with textured cardboard; and a carpet-covered post on its own stand.

Cat door: this model is hinged . . .

to push outwards . . .

CAT DOOR

It is important that pet cats should have access to the house at all times during the day and night. If they are unable to get into their own home and bed whenever they want, cats are likely to wander off for long periods, getting involved in fights with other cats, and at great risk of being injured by traffic, or even stolen. Eventually these unwanted cats seek another home elsewhere with a more friendly family.

A cat door, fitted into one of the external doors of the house, is a useful aid. It provides a cat with an easy means of access to the house, and the cat doors are made in such a way that they are burglar-proof if fitted correctly. They measure about 15 cm/6 in square, and should be fixed out of reach of the security locks and bolts.

Some cat doors may be opened by the cat itself by means of a radio-controlled device fitted to a safety collar, and these doors are ideal, if your cat does not object to the collar, for use in areas where stray cats may decide to check your cat's home for food.

Some models have two-way flaps, as illustrated here; with others the cat needs to lift it up to return. Many can be adjusted so that your cat can come in, but not go out again – a useful refinement if you do not want your cat to go out at night.

or inwards

It is easy for children to become over-excited by the arrival of a new pet. Special care should be taken to treat it very gently while it makes itself at home.

Settling in

Whereas it is a fairly simple matter to introduce a young kitten to its new home and to a new family and pets, it is a little more difficult with an adult cat. Cats are such creatures of habit that they do not take kindly to any change of home or routine. Because of this, it is necessary to make proper preparation before introducing a cat to your house.

First, decide where you will keep the cat until it has made friends with you, your family and other pets, if you have them. Make sure that the room or area is escape-proof and

that there are no spaces into which the cat may crawl to hide, and possibly get trapped. Cats can and do squeeze into remarkably small holes – the back of a boiler for instance – and many cats have hidden in chimneys. Provide the new cat with a litter tray, and a set of food and water bowls. Make sure that the bed you select is cosy and warm and that the cat will feel safe and secure in it amidst the strange surroundings of its new home.

Make a great fuss of your new pet, constantly using its name, and it will soon show its acceptance of you by scent marking you, rubbing its forehead and lips against your hands and legs. When this happens, and you are confident that the cat will come to you, you may make your first excursions to other parts of the house, and eventually into the garden.

Children must be taught to handle the cat correctly, and to treat it with respect at all times. Resident pets may not immediately accept a new cat into the home, and great care must be exercised while the newcomer is being introduced. Resident pets must not be made to feel jealous and the new addition must not feel threatened or intimidated. If you can borrow a kitten pen, the new cat may be popped in this while your other pets are first introduced, to guard against possible fights.

Animals meeting for the first time are understandably wary of each other, but with patience they will usually tolerate each other – or even become good friends.

Feeding

Cats are by nature predatory animals, catching mice, young rats, birds, and sometimes fish and amphibians with great stealth and skill.

Their method is to lie in wait for their victim, or to stalk it up to the moment of the final pounce. The shortness of the muzzle makes it difficult for the cat to reach out and snap at the prey with the jaws. Instead their style is to bring down the prey with the paws, and to deliver the death blow with the teeth. This handling makes it appear the cat is playing with its prey.

Hunting ability is to some extent a matter of heredity, some cats being notoriously better than others. Those which are well fed and in peak condition are likely to be better hunters than others, and only cats in prime condition are able to tackle a rat.

This hunting instinct cannot be erased from the cat's nature, but bird-lovers should avoid enticing birds into the cat's territory with food, nest boxes and so on.

The best mousers are well-fed cats in good condition, descended from a line of skilled hunters.

Being creatures of habit, cats appreciate a regular routine.

An adult cat needs about 50 kilocalories per 450g/1lb of body weight per day. A sedentary neutered cat may keep fit on a little less, and a very active cat may require a little more, while a lactating female's requirement may be as high as 125–150 kilocalories per 450g/1lb of her body-weight while feeding an average litter of four kittens.

Most cats seem to thrive best on two regular daily meals, but old cats may need smaller meals at more frequent intervals, rather like young kittens. In some cases, old cats with kidney disease or constipation may require special diets and veterinary advice should be sought.

There may be a tendency for neutered animals to put on excess weight with age, but this should be controlled with a little adjustment to the diet. Cut out all cereal and milk and feed good quality, high-protein, low-fat meals in small quantities.

Your cat's general appearance will tell you whether or not you are feeding correctly. An obese cat is obviously having too much food, while a thin cat is either having too little food or is suffering from internal parasites.

Signs that the cat's diet is lacking in certain nutrients include a dry, scurfy coat, a warm, dry nose, dull eyes, flaking claws, offensive faeces and bad breath.

Nutritional requirements for a healthy cat

Proteins   At least 25 per cent of an adult cat's diet should consist of protein; 35–40 per cent if it is a breeding pedigree. Protein is found in muscle meat, fish, eggs, cheese and milk. Cats must have some protein of animal origin. Unlike humans and, with care, dogs, they cannot maintain good health on a vegetarian diet. Cats which cannot digest milk may be able to cope with plain yoghurt.

Fats   Cats can digest a high proportion of fats in their diet and up to 25 per cent fat is recommended by feline nutritionists for young, growing cats. Fats provide concentrated forms of energy, and contain fatty acids which promote healthy skin and coats. Fats also contain fat-soluble vitamins A, D, E and K. Fats are present in some meat, butter, margarine and cooking oils.

Offering your cat a varied, but predominantly meat-based, diet will ensure it receives all the nutrients necessary for good health.

Carbohydrates   Cooked grains and pulses are sometimes fed to cats to bulk out a protein-rich diet, but are not necessary for a cat's well-being.

Vitamins and minerals   Cats fed a varied, well-balanced diet will obtain all the vitamins and minerals they require. Vitamin/mineral supplements should not be given without veterinary advice.

Vitamin A: A cat's requirement for this vitamin can be supplied by feeding a good general diet and adding 28 g/ 1 oz of lightly cooked liver on one day per week. Too much vitamin A can be dangerous, leading to laying down of excess bone in the spine.

Vitamin B group: The B vitamins may be destroyed by cooking and so select canned foods in which these vitamins have been replaced in processing.

Vitamin C: Generally considered unnecessary for cats except when recovering from illness or having antibiotic treatment. It can be administered in the orange-flavoured syrup sold for human babies.

Vitamins D and E: The cat's needs are low compared to those of the dog, or man, and are provided in a normal diet.

A feeding guide

Age	Average body weight kg/lb	Daily food requirements g/oz	Number of meals per day
5 months	2kg/4½lb	170g/6oz	3
7–8 months	3kg/6½lb	200g/7oz	2–3
Adult	4–4.5kg/9–10lb	185–225g/ 6½oz–8oz	1–2
Pregnant female	3.5kg/7½lb	250g/8½oz	2–3
Lactating female	2.5kg/5½lb	400g/14oz	4

FRESH FOOD
A butcher or fishmonger will supply good but inexpensive fresh meat and fish suitable for feeding raw, and offal which must be cooked. Always feed a variety of food for best nutritional balance, and remember that cheap meat is as good, nutritionally, as expensive meat.

Avoid bones that may splinter or lodge in the throat.

Cats take a little vegetable matter directly in the wild, and some indirectly by eating the stomach contents of their prey. In captivity very small amounts of vegetable or cereal, such as wholemeal bread, may be added to their diet as a source of roughage.

CONVENIENCE FOODS
More expensive, but ready-prepared meals are available as canned or packeted cat food. These should be fed exactly according to the manufacturer's instructions.

Dehydrated cat foods must always be given with large quantities of drinking water. Without this a cat may sometimes develop a urinary tract infection.

DRINKING WATER AND MILK
Many cats prefer to drink from a dripping tap or puddle, rather than from their own water bowl, but fresh drinking water must nevertheless be provided. Chemical-tasting tap water can be made more palatable with the addition of a little meat or fish stock.

Cats also like milk, but it is not a necessary source of nutrition for an adult. Too much milk in a diet can lead to obesity, and overweight cats can often be slimmed by having their milk ration reduced.

Grooming

SHORT-HAIRED CATS

The cat's own tongue is a well-adapted tool for grooming its natural, i.e. short-haired coat. Strictly speaking, there is no need for owners to groom short-haired cats for most of the year, although brushing does keep the cat tractable, and allows close examination of its condition.

When a short-haired cat is moulting the owner's attention is vital. During moulting an ungroomed cat will swallow loose hairs, some of which may become lodged in the digestive tract, and become matted with food to form hard balls. These hair balls might cause serious blockages, and may need veterinary attention.

Cats normally moult twice a year, but moulting is frequently prolonged by poor feeding or by ill-health.

Most short-haired cats benefit greatly from the regular use of a very fine-toothed comb. This effectively removes loose and dead hair from the coat, dead flakes of skin, and if fleas are present, the comb will catch them and also remove the dark flecks of their excreta.

If cats swallow hair they will eat grass as an emetic, to make themselves vomit. For this reason grass should always be available to them. City cats will perhaps need to have some grown in a flower pot.

Siamese cat demonstrating the use of the tongue as a most effective tool for grooming

LONG-HAIRED CATS

Long-haired cats are quite unable to groom themselves adequately. Their long fur is the result of breeding from long-haired mutants that would probably have died out in the wild. No wild cat has hair of this length; no cat is capable of grooming it by himself.

Daily grooming is absolutely essential for all long-haired breeds, and many experienced fanciers recommend two or even three grooming periods a day. Any burr, small twig, or fragment of dead leaf will otherwise quickly become the centre of a tangle that will have to be cut out. In extreme cases, the badly matted long-haired cat may need to be anaesthetized by the veterinary surgeon for de-matting.

Grass is used as an emetic. City cats with no access to a grassy area will need a turf or grass grown in a flower pot.

From a very early age long-haired cats will need to become accustomed to being brushed out and combed every day as a matter of routine. At first, care must be taken not to overtax the kitten's patience.

Bathing is not necessary, although some white cats like bathing, notably the Turkish Van cats. There are also dry shampoos available for occasional use.

Short-haired cats need grooming during a moult. For this reason they should be accustomed to being brushed from a young age.

Those which are not brushed when shedding hair are in danger of swallowing so much that it becomes matted with food to form hair balls.

These hair balls may cause serious blockage, and need removing by surgery.

Long-haired cats are quite incapable of grooming themselves adequately, and need to be brushed and combed at least once daily throughout the year.

The long-haired coat does not occur in the wild, and the cat's tongue, although normally an efficient grooming tool, is not effective on long hair.

Unless groomed daily these cats may develop a seriously matted coat.

Burmese

British Black

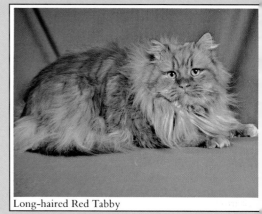

Long-haired Red Tabby

Long-haired Tortoiseshell and White

Chartreux

Birman Seal Point

Handling and training

When lifting a cat place one hand beneath the chest and the other around the hind legs so that the entire weight is supported. If the cat is immediately turned towards the handler it will be able to cling to clothing for extra security. Never pick a cat up by the scruff of the neck, since this is too great a strain on all but very young kittens. Similarly it is wrong to pick up a cat by the front quarters only, allowing the hind legs to hang down.

Cats should be accustomed to being handled correctly from an early age, and to having all parts of the body touched, whether or not this is at grooming time. It is a good idea to institute a regular routine for checking the cat's coat behind the ears and along the spine for signs of fleas; gently cleaning inside the ear-flaps, and extending the claws to check for injuries. Children must be taught to respect the cat, and to handle it gently and safely.

Handling: support the weight.

In an emergency: use a blanket.

EMERGENCY HANDLING
It may be impossible to handle a cat normally in an emergency, for instance after a road accident, because it will scratch out in terror at anyone who goes near it. The safest method is to drop a blanket on to the cat and wrap it round firmly with just the head free. In this way it can safely be transported to a veterinary surgeon.

When rescuing a trapped cat it would be wise to wear strong gloves to protect the hands, and as soon as possible take hold of the cat's front paws to prevent their scratching the face. Holding a cat by the scruff of the neck will help to prevent your being bitten.

PET CARRIERS
When it happens that a cat needs to be moved from the house to be taken to the veterinary surgeon, cattery, pet show, or on holiday, it must always be secured in a box. Any strong cardboard box with a safe base will serve as a carrier. Air holes need to be punched in the sides and string tied securely to form a handle.

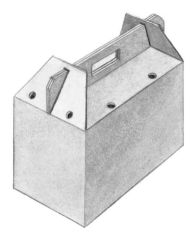

Cardboard pet carrier

TRAINING

It is important to choose a simple, effective name for your cat and to make sure that it identifies with its name by constant use, particularly at feeding and petting times.

Never use the cat's name in a cross way. Scolding is best done by sharp clapping of the hands when the cat is caught in the act of misbehaving, and rewards for good behaviour can consist of cat 'treats' or titbits, or stroking in the cat's favourite way.

Both scolding and rewards must be given at the time of the behaviour needing correction or fixing, otherwise the cat will be unable to connect your behavioural response with its own.

Cats are very sensitive and will never forgive or forget being smacked. They do not like being shouted at either, but you might find a low, growling 'no' works well when your cat is seen to be doing something unacceptable. You may also lightly grasp the loose skin at the scruff of the neck and give a little shake, rather as a mother cat does to its kittens.

On the whole, cats will accept very basic 'training' but may or may not do as you want, when you want it. They are all very independent creatures and will never perform tricks to order.

Cats soon learn to recognize their owner's voice.

Exercise

It is a characteristic of the entire cat family that, although they are capable of short bursts of energy, they do not have the dog's stamina for sustained exercise. In many ways this makes them very suitable household pets, because they are content to spend a great deal of time resting.

So far as possible cats should be encouraged to stay near their own house and garden, and this is not impossible with cats that have been neutered. Tom cats which have been castrated will have less desire to roam than entire cats, and similarly females which have been spayed will not be so restless, nor will they entice toms to the house with their calling.

Even if the family cat is not free to exercise at will, it is obvious that any cat should have the freedom to play in its own garden every day. The cat will be most content if the garden is rather wild, with trees for it to climb and bushes to stalk through. In particular, cats like a high vantage point from which to survey their territory, and will often climb on to a roof-top to secure one. Although a cat will find its way through any fence or over any wall, neutered cats usually stay within 'their' territory.

COLLARS AND LEADS

It is even possible to exercise some breeds of cat on a lead. Many of the Orientals, and in particular the Siamese, will wear a cat collar comfortably and allow themselves to be led by their owner.

It might seem that a cat collar, used with a name disc, is an excellent way of identifying a cat in case of mishap, but this is not always so. Any collar used should be made wholly or partly of elastic 1cm/½in wide that will stretch enough for the cat to slip its head through if the collar ever becomes caught up on a branch or railing. Unfortunately even this safety precaution is not completely satisfactory. A cat trapped in a tree by its own collar will struggle and may twist the collar into a figure of eight shape until it becomes a noose.

Orientals may walk on a lead.

A collar could become a noose.

Given a garden to roam in freely, a cat will soon discover its favourite vantage point from which to survey its territory.

INDOOR GAMES

Cats kept entirely in the house must be given lots of play and exercise opportunities, otherwise they soon become lazy, lethargic and possibly overweight. You should set aside a period for playtime each day and encourage your cat to chase after a feather on a string, ping-pong balls or cat toys suitable for tossing around the room. Some cats become adept at retrieving, and you will tire of the game long before your feline friend. Large cardboard boxes can be stuck together with non-toxic glue and have interconnecting holes cut through to form a maze. Cats love leaping into boxes, hiding and pouncing out through the different holes.

Wooden step ladders can be converted into the ideal climbing toys for housebound cats; carpet offcuts can be tacked or stuck to the treads and a padded cushion fixed to the topmost step. Some of the larger firms of pet product manufacturers sell wonderful carpet-covered 'cat trees' which fit from floor to ceiling of the average room. Cats love to shin up the 'trunk' and use the various 'branches' for sitting, or sleeping. Some of the cat trees have hollow drums at the bottom for holding a removable toilet tray, or the cat's bed. There are all manner of sophisticated toys and feline furniture, designed expressly for confined cats, and though many of the items are expensive, they do last for many years and provide endless hours of exercise and fun.

Travelling and boarding

Whenever you take your cat anywhere by car you should confine it within a suitable, comfortable carrier. An unconfined cat can be a hazard when driving and may run off when the car door is opened.

To habituate your cat to its carrier, start putting your cat into the basket at odd times. Make sure there is a soft blanket inside and perhaps a favourite toy. It is best to carry out carrier training just before feeding time, then the cat comes to regard the carrier as leading to good things. If you habitually make very long journeys, get a carrier or cage large enough to contain a small litter tray and hook-on food and water containers, as well as your cat's cushion or blanket. Cat carriers range from sturdy wooden crates designed for air travel to fold-out cardboard containers suitable only for emergency use. In between there are wicker baskets of several different designs, some of which convert to beds by removing the front wire grill. Plastic-covered wire-mesh carriers are very secure and easily cleaned. Cats like them because they can see out and do not feel too constrained within them. There are also many designs made in plastic and fibreglass.

RSPCA cattery at Chobham, Surrey, where cats are housed securely in individual cat cabins, each with its own enclosed run, litter tray, and ramp to an elevated sleeping section that contains the bed.

Apart from using space to best effect, the elevated section and its ramp satisfies the cat's natural desire to climb up above ground level.

Cats fluff out their thick winter coat for added insulation in cold weather and wrap their tail round as a muffler. Providing the cat has a good, draughtproof bed, heating is not normally advisable, but in RSPCA catteries it is available for use in very severe weather, and for old, sick or delicate cats.

WHEN YOU ARE AWAY

At holiday time it may be possible to arrange for a friend, neighbour or relative to visit the house two or three times a day to tend to the cat. This is probably the best method of all, since cats prefer to remain in their own home, and although they may miss the family, at least their own surroundings are unchanged.

It is not a good idea to move the cat into somebody else's home, from which it will immediately try to escape. Neither is it possible to leave the cat alone to find its own food. This is both cruel and illegal, and classed as abandonment in law.

The alternative is to arrange for the cat to board at a good cattery. At RSPCA catteries the cats have their own cabins, which are very secure and have a covered run, litter tray and an elevated sleeping section with heater. This is approached by a ramp, and the cat enters by way of a cat door.

Any cattery will need as much notice as possible, and will want to see an up-to-date vaccination certificate. No good cattery would accept a cat which had not been inoculated against the major infectious cat diseases.

A cat should never be left to fend for itself while its owners are away on holiday.

Wicker-baskets make secure and long-lasting carriers.

The healthy cat

Most cats are extremely healthy and resilient, with such quick reflexes and good agility that they survive, with their legendary 'nine lives', in situations where slower animals would perish. Getting to know your cat well will help you recognize quickly any deterioration in condition or change in behaviour.

A healthy, alert cat

A cat's natural resistance to disease is lowered by cold, damp living conditions and poor food. Like humans, they can suffer from the malfunction of certain organs, such as the heart, kidneys and liver, and the best guard against this is prevention.

Ensure your cat receives a good, varied diet (pp.18-21). A faddy eater may not be taking in sufficient nutrition to keep him in tip-top condition, and a cat which habitually drinks too little can be prone to kidney and digestive troubles later on in life.

A cat cooped up indoors alone all day soon becomes either frustrated and destructive or bored and lazy. Lack of exercise coupled with the wrong food can lead to obesity, which in turn can lead to a variety of health problems.

Even if a cat is accustomed to going out at night, and is too old to change the habit of a lifetime, it must always have access – perhaps by way of a cat door (p.15) – to a dry, warm retreat, particularly as the cat begins to age.

Infectious diseases may be transmitted in several ways: through droplets sneezed, coughed or breathed out by the infected cat, which are then breathed in by a susceptible cat, or through contaminated drink, feeding bowls or bedding. Flies, fleas or other agents, with faeces, urine, vomit, pus or saliva can pass on disease from an infected cat, or illness may be passed by direct contact between cats which live together.

SYMPTOMS OF DISEASE
The first symptom of disease in the cat is generally loss of appetite, either partially or completely, and when this happens the caring owner will immediately look for the

cause. Most cats eagerly await their regular meals and consume the entire contents of the dish within minutes. Some cats are more finicky, but any change in the cat's normal eating pattern should be treated as a warning sign.

Other signs of the onset of an illness are indicated by changes in the cat's appearance or behaviour. It may sit hunched up or resent being touched. It may sit over its water bowl but seem unable to drink. It may go repeatedly to its toilet tray but seem unable to pass either urine or faeces. The eyes may look dull, or the third eyelid appear like a skin at the inner corners of the eyes. The cat may stop washing and its fur become odorous. Its breath may smell foul or it might sneeze, drool, vomit or have diarrhoea. When contacting the veterinary surgeon, be sure to list all the symptoms and the order of their onset to help him make an accurate diagnosis.

SIGNS OF HEALTH

Abdomen	without wounds, growths, and sores; not distended or unduly sensitive.
Anus	clean, with no staining or scouring; motions passed without persistent constipation or diarrhoea.
Appetite	good; weight maintained in adults, and growth in kittens; no persistent vomiting.
Breathing	even and quiet, with no wheezing or coughing.
Coat	clean, well-groomed, glossy; free from parasites, their eggs and faeces, loose hairs and scurviness. No baldness or patches.
Claws	no splits, thorns, splinters or damaged pads.
Demeanour	watchful, even at rest; quickly responsive to sounds; quiet and contented.
Ears	pricked to catch sounds; free of discharge; no irritation, scratching or shaking of head.
Eyes	clear, not bloodshot; third eyelid not showing; no discharge or watering.
Faeces	droppings buried, except sometimes by toms marking territory as dogs do. No persistent constipation or diarrhoea.
Movement	free movement, agile, with no stiffness in joints or gait. Weight evenly distributed.
Skin	supple, with no scurf, inflammation, parasites or sores.
Teeth and gums	clean teeth, free of tartar; gums pink, not inflamed, white or yellowish.
Urine	passed effortlessly, with no pain. Normal for toms to spray in house and garden to mark territory, as dogs do.

Vaccinations

Although there is a whole range of illnesses that a cat may suffer, some of the more serious infectious cat diseases can be prevented by a programme of routine vaccinations. Very effective vaccines are available to protect against feline infectious enteritis and feline upper respiratory disease (FURD), commonly known as feline influenza or 'cat flu'. Depending on the make of vaccine, injections may be started in the young kitten from 8, 10 or 12 weeks, with booster doses being given on veterinary advice. It is usual to have adult cats boosted at regular intervals, usually annually or every two years. If it is to be boarded or, if a breeding queen, sent away for mating, it is important to have your cat's vaccinations and boosters given in good time, as immunity may not be complete for several days after the injections.

Cats should have a certificate recording details of their vaccinations. If you are not sure when your cat was last immunized your vet will begin a programme of boosters which should be continued throughout the cat's life.

A veterinary surgeon is experienced at keeping pets calm and unfrightened by a visit to the surgery.

Major infectious diseases

Vaccinations provide effective immunization against the following diseases:

FELINE INFECTIOUS ENTERITIS

This is a common virus disease with symptoms of abdominal pain, vomiting and collapse. The cat suffers severe dehydration, and although obviously thirsty, will not be able to drink. Once the disease is contracted, it is almost impossible to effect a cure and immunization is the only real safeguard. This disease spreads rapidly among cats, and kittens are especially vulnerable.

FELINE INFLUENZA

An infectious disease common in summer time, 'cat flu' is caused by a group of viruses affecting the upper respiratory tract, with symptoms of sneezing, running eyes and nose, and excessive salivation. Prompt veterinary treatment can usually cure feline influenza but cats frequently become carriers. This is one reason why vaccination is essential to protect your own and other cats.

There are also some less common but serious infectious diseases for which no vaccine is as yet commercially available.

Feline leukaemia is now known to be caused by a virus (FeLV) spread by saliva, urine and faeces. It is not as contagious as other common feline diseases and seems mainly to be spread by close contact over a long period of time. A preventative vaccine is being developed.

Feline infectious peritonitis (FIP), inflammation of the peritoneum or lining of the abdomen, has a variety of causes. It is a serious condition for which there is at present no cure.

Recently a virus has been discovered which causes an auto-immune deficiency syndrome in cats (**FIV**). A blood test is available and your vet will advise you. The virus is not infectious to humans.

Ailments

DIGESTIVE PROBLEMS

A cat will regulate any minor digestive disorders by eating grass to make itself sick. Occasional constipation can be relieved by a tablespoonful of medicinal paraffin or olive oil, but consult the vet if it continues for more than a couple of days. Diarrhoea can be caused by too much milk or be a symptom of a number of more serious ailments. Try feeding beaten egg white or a little boiled rice. Again, trouble persisting for more than a day or so should be referred to the veterinary surgeon.

EARS

A number of irritants can cause cats to scratch persistently at their ears. It could be ear mites (for which your vet can supply drops), a small seed which has worked its way into the ear, or an abscessed wound inflicted by another cat. As a cat's ear is extremely delicate and vulnerable, seek help from the vet rather than attempting to solve the problem yourself.

HAIR BALLS

Long-haired cats, if not meticulously groomed, will suffer from hair balls from time to time. By ingesting their own hair in the course of grooming themselves, a clot of matted hair will form in the gut. Usually a cat will solve the problem itself by chewing grass, but severe cases may need an operation.

SKIN COMPLAINTS

If small spots or sore patches appear on your cat's skin, do not attempt to treat them yourself with ointments or shampoos, as similar-looking conditions may be due to a variety of sources, such as parasites (p.38), an allergic reaction or may be symptomatic of an internal disorder. Eczema, showing as a raw-looking red inflammation of the skin, may be caused by too much fish in the diet or, on a neutered cat, to a hormone imbalance. Your vet will advise.

STINGS

Cats often play with bees and wasps until they sustain their first sting. This usually teaches them to avoid buzzing insects in the future. A single sting is painful, but not dangerous unless it is inside the mouth or in the throat. Remove the sting if present and apply a cold water compress or ice pack if possible. If the swelling does not go down in a few hours, consult your veterinary surgeon.

TEETH AND GUMS

Some cats are more prone than others to build-up of tartar around the base of the teeth. Left unchecked, this can lead to gingivitis (painful inflammation of the gums) and eventual loss of teeth. Bad breath and difficulty in eating are warning signs. Your vet will need to scrape off the tartar, since it is extremely hard and cats do not take to having their teeth cleaned! Encouraging your cat to eat biscuity 'cat treats' will help to prevent a build-up recurring.

ZOONOSES

Zoonoses are diseases capable of spreading between animals and humans, but luckily there are very few. The most deadly zoonosis is **rabies**, controlled in the United Kingdom and a few other countries, by stringent quarantine laws. (In the United Kingdom, inoculation against rabies is only permitted by the Ministry of Agriculture for animals which are to be exported.)

Toxoplasmosis is a serious zoonosis, caused by a microscopic organism called *Toxoplasma*. This parasite can affect many animals, but only the cat spreads the infective cysts by voiding them in its faeces. A cat with the disease may show no symptoms, but the disease may cause congenital defects in a pregnant woman's unborn baby. The normal way to prevent toxoplasmosis in the cat is to feed only heat-processed and well-cooked fresh meat, and to ensure that the cat does not catch or eat wild prey. Always wash your hands after handling raw meat, or fondling the cat, and pregnant women should avoid changing cats' litter trays.

Ringworm is a fungus infection which may cause characteristic lesions on the skin. It is important that a cat with ringworm should be taken for veterinary examination and treated immediately, particularly because it is readily transmissible to man. Do not allow a child any contact whatsoever with a cat showing symptoms of ringworm, since children are most at risk of cross-infection.

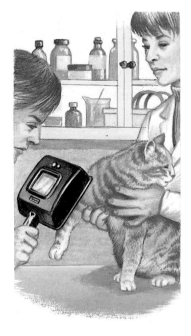

Inspecting for ringworm.

Parasites

Cat flea

FLEAS
Well-kept cats from very clean homes can pick up fleas from time to time. Use a flea powder or aerosol flea spray to treat the cat's coat, following the manufacturer's instructions.

This treatment alone will not clear up an infestation of fleas. It is also necessary to clean the cat's bedding, and to scrub his bed and all his haunts. The essential point is that fleas do not lay the eggs on his fur but on his bedding and surroundings, and unless these are cleaned thoroughly the infestation will continue.

It is advisable to treat a cat for fleas at the same time as it is wormed, because the two infestations may be linked.

LICE
Cats may also be affected by lice that are more difficult to see than fleas, although their white eggs, or nits, show up well, particularly on dark fur. Cats that constantly lick and bite themselves may be infested with lice, and should be taken to a veterinary surgeon for examination. The veterinary surgeon will be able to prescribe a good spray that will need to be used for at least a month.

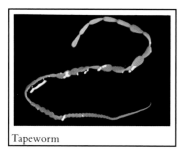
Tapeworm

WORMS
Both roundworms and tapeworms can affect cats. An infestation of roundworms may cause diarrhoea, loss of weight, and poor condition. Sometimes these worms are vomited. Tapeworms seldom cause any such symptoms, but segments of the worms can be seen around the anus of an infected cat.

All kittens should be treated for roundworms as a matter of routine. The necessary tablets can be obtained from a chemist or from a veterinary surgeon. Administration is simple, but care must be taken to give the correct dosage. Tapeworm treatments are more difficult to administer, and if an infestation is suspected, then veterinary help must be sought.

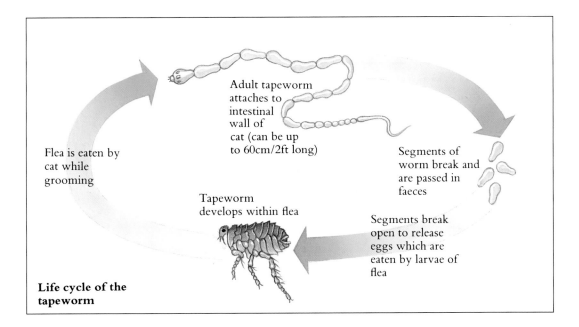

Adult tapeworm attaches to intestinal wall of cat (can be up to 60cm/2ft long)

Flea is eaten by cat while grooming

Segments of worm break and are passed in faeces

Tapeworm develops within flea

Segments break open to release eggs which are eaten by larvae of flea

Life cycle of the tapeworm

EAR MITES
Ear mites cause a great deal of suffering to cats and especially to kittens. Symptoms of ear trouble are scratching the ears, shaking or banging the head, and a brown encrustation within the ear canal. A veterinary surgeon should be consulted without delay, and will prescribe a treatment for the condition.

MANGE MITES
Cats can also be affected by a mite which causes skin canker with early symptoms of small bare patches on the ears and face. This can develop into a very serious skin condition unless treated by a veterinary surgeon in the early stages.

TICKS
Cats are more likely to be found with ticks in some areas than in others. The ticks sink their head-parts into the cat's skin and engorge themselves by sucking the cat's blood. In a few days, when fully engorged, they drop off. It is not possible to remove a live tick completely with a pair of tweezers, as the head-part will remain firmly embedded. The ticks can be killed however, by cutting off their air supply for about 30 minutes with a smear of butter or something similar. Once dead they can be pulled off cleanly with the tweezers.

Administering medicine

ADMINISTERING MEDICATION

If a cat becomes nervous and needs to be restrained, it is best to wrap a towel around him.

The method of opening up the cat's mouth is to rest one hand on the top of his head and press the thumb and forefinger against the angles of his jaws. First lower the head and then raise it and there will be a small gap between the jaws at the front.

ADMINISTERING TABLETS

A tablet held between the thumb and forefinger of the free hand can be inserted as shown, pushed well back on the tongue. Alternatively use a pill applicator manufactured specially for animals.

ADMINISTERING LIQUID MEDICINE

If the mouth is opened as described there will be sufficient space at the front of the jaws to allow liquid medicine to be trickled off a spoon, a few drops at a time. Lower the head to allow the cat to swallow, and repeat until the dose has been given. Alternatively adminster liquid medicine with a small plastic syringe.

ADMINISTERING EAR DROPS

Since ear trouble can occur among cats, a veterinary surgeon may have to prescribe ear drops at some time. Hold the cat's head to one side, and insert the drops from their own applicator into the ear canal, gently massaging behind the ear to allow the drops to penetrate as far as possible. Clean away any discharge from the ear with great care.

ADMINISTERING EYE DROPS

When eye drops are prescribed, hold the cat's head back, and drop in the lotion from its own applicator to the inner corner of the eye. Hold the head back for a moment or two, while the drops run over the whole eye surface.

First aid

If your cat is unfortunate enough to sustain a major injury, call the veterinary surgery immediately to ensure that someone will be there. There are several things you can do while waiting for veterinary help.

Make sure the cat is able to breath without obstruction, which might necessitate the clearing of the airway. To do this, pull the tongue forward, gripping it gently with a piece of rough cloth or towelling – a face flannel is ideal. Take care not to get bitten in the process.

Any heavy bleeding should be staunched by placing a clean folded handkerchief or tea towel over the wound and applying enough pressure to stop the blood flow.

Shock is countered by keeping the cat warm and quiet in a darkened room. Cover with a blanket and apply a well-wrapped hot-water bottle, or raise the temperature of the room overall.

If the cat appears to have sustained a fracture, do not move unless absolutely necessary. Never attempt to apply any form of splint.

If you suspect fractures, and the cat must be moved, it is best to slide it carefully on to a flat tray or board, which can then be used as an effective stretcher. If there are no fractures, lift the cat carefully into a secure carrier.

If you have to give initial treatment to a wound yourself, bathe it with warm water, attempting to remove all superficial dirt. When the wound looks clean, bathe it again with saline solution made by dissolving one teaspoon of ordinary table salt in half a litre/1 pint of cooled boiled water. Do not use any disinfectant or antiseptic on the wound and leave it unbandaged until it has been professionally treated.

If poisoning is suspected, seek immediate veterinary advice, taking the packet or a sample of the poison you think has been taken. Treat as for shock.

A small burn or scald can be cooled by immersion in cold water until help is at hand. Otherwise wrap the animal in a clean tea towel, sheet or pillowslip to exclude the air, and seek immediate veterinary help.

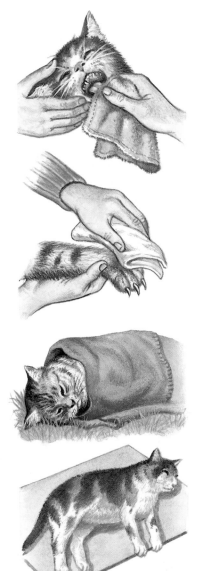

Reproduction

MATING

Unfortunately most matings between cats are unplanned. They are, however, almost invariably successful. The female cat ovulates in response to a male and there are, therefore, always eggs ready to be fertilized.

Siamese Lilac Point with kittens

OESTRUS

Female cats are capable of breeding from the age of about six months. In practice they usually come into season in the first spring after the age of six months. They do not have a regular oestrous cycle, but come into season repeatedly throughout the year until they are mated. Whilst they are on heat they adopt an unmistakable pattern of behaviour which includes restless searching for a tom, and also calling toms to the house. The Foreign breeds, in particular, are very vocal at this time.

PREGNANCY

Pregnancy last approximately nine weeks, within the limits of sixty to sixty-five days. For the first five weeks of pregnancy the queen will need no special attention, but her abdomen should not be handled carelessly. During the last month of pregnancy, when the kittens show, her appetite will increase markedly and she should be allowed as much good food as she will eat. In addition a daily vitamin/ mineral tablet will be a useful supplement.

KITTENING

A pet cat should be allowed to have her kittens in the house. She will accept a box provided for her if it is a comfortable size, and placed in a dark corner where it will be warm and dry and easy for her to reach even when heavily pregnant. It should be lined thickly with newspapers that can be burned and replaced after the litter has been born.

It is unusual for a cat to need help during birth. She will

herself clean the kittens, eat the placentas, and guide each kitten in turn to a teat for suckling.

THE TOM CAT

The queen alone is responsible for the kittens, needing no help other than some praise from an understanding owner, and good food. Sometimes, when there are two queens in the household, one will help the other.

The tom should not be allowed access to the kittens before they are four months old. While they are very young they are at risk, and kittens are quite frequently killed by the tom, especially when they are being raised in an outbuilding or shed, and have no human protection.

KITTENS' NEEDS

Kittens open their eyes between 5 and 10 days and continue to suckle from the queen to the age of 7–8 weeks. At three weeks of age the litter starts to take an interest in their mother's food dish and the most precocious will try eating solids. The kittens can be tempted to try baby cereals with evaporated milk, scrambled egg, and cooked, flaked white fish or cooked minced chicken with the skin removed.

SURPLUS KITTENS

The queen will come into season again immediately after giving birth which means that she could give birth to three litters a year, with an average of six kittens to each litter. Kittens can be very difficult to home, and if the whole litter cannot be kept or re-homed then the surplus kittens must be destroyed humanely.

Drowning is very cruel death, and cannot be recommended even for very young kittens. Instead they should be taken to a veterinary surgeon, or to an RSPCA Inspector who will destroy them humanely.

Your questions answered

Our garden backs on to farmland and our three cats are always bringing in 'presents' of mice and voles. Short of moving, what can we do to stop them?

It is impossible to subdue your cats' natural hunting instincts. Unless your pets are confined to the house, which is not advised, they will continue to present you with trophies of their hunts. Town cats may not prey on rodents, but they are likely to bring home birds – sometimes quite large ones – or take to fishing in a neighbour's goldfish pond instead, so even moving is not a solution.

Constant scolding will not help either: a cat can be trained not to scratch the furniture or urinate indoors, but you will never persuade it to change its predatory nature. Old age and laziness are the only real deterrents!

I have heard that cats can be a danger to new babies. Is this true?

There have been reports of babies being smothered by cats which, presumably attracted by the warmth, have settled down to sleep on the cot pillow. These accidents are happily very rare, and could have been prevented by the simple expedient of fitting a special 'cat' net to the pram or over the cot when there are cats in the family. No small baby should ever be left alone with any pet, and strict standards of hygiene must be observed at all times.

My long-coated cat seems to swallow a lot of her fur when she is licking herself, and it sometimes makes her very sick. Is it doing her any harm?

Long-coated cats often take in quantities of their own fur while grooming themselves and this can lead to the formation of 'hairballs' when the hair compacts into a solid mass. This leads to digestive problems, as the hairball is either vomited or causes a blockage in the intestines.

As prevention is better than cure, be sure to groom your cat each day, removing all the loose hairs, then finish off by passing a slightly damp cloth over the cat's coat. Daily combing and brushing will also prevent the formation of dense mats of fur which have to be cut out.

We are shortly moving and I would like to know how best to settle my old cat into his new home.
The bustle and disruption of moving day would be bewildering to any cat, which may run off in fright to hide before the removal van has even arrived. To avoid frantic searches at the last minute, keep your cat indoors with a litter tray the night before, possibly in a room which has already been cleared, so that he need not be disturbed. He should travel – *not* in the removal van – in a secure pet carrier (see p. 30 for suggestions for a long journey) and, to begin with, be confined to one room in the new house, furnished with things with which he is familiar. Possessions are important to cats, so make sure you take with you your pet's bed, bedding and toys. Keep your cat indoors for several days, providing a litter tray, gradually introducing him to more rooms. Eventually, take him into the garden prior to feeding time. Let him have a good sniff around, then bring him indoors for a favourite meal. After a few such excursions it will be safe to let your cat out alone, as he will have accepted the new house and garden, and will have learned his way around.

Can cats really see in the dark?
Though cats have very good eyesight and can adjust their pupils to see clearly in very dim conditions, they are unable to see in complete darkness.

I have heard that cats are fond of catnip. What is this and where can I get some?
Catnip is the dried leaves of the *Nepeta cataria*, or catmint, and some cats (not all) find the smell almost intoxicating. You can grow your own, or dried catnip can be bought in sachets from pet shops or by mail order and can be used in cushions and soft toys. Some cat toys and scratching posts are impregnated with catnip, and if your cat is one of those attracted by the smell, it acts as an attractive aid to training.

I recently saw a cat wearing a sort of plastic ruff. Was this just some unkind dressing up, or was there a reason for it?
What you saw was a veterinary device known as an Elizabethan collar. These are used to prevent cats from biting at wounds or removing stitches from recent operations.

Life history

Scientific name	*Felis catus*
Gestation period	63 days (approx.)
Litter size	3–5 (average)
Birth weight	90g/3oz–140g/5oz
Eyes open	5–10 days
Weaning age	42-49 days
Weaning weight	500g/1lb 2oz–650g/1lb 7oz
Puberty	120–180 days
Adult weight	males 3.5kg/8lb–5.9kg/13lb females 2.25kg/5lb–3kg/7lb
Best age to breed	12+ months
Oestrus (or season)	Repeatedly in season unless mated
Duration of oestrus	7–14 days
Retire from breeding	males 10 years females 8 years
Life expectancy	12–16 years

Record card

Record sheet for your own cat

Name _____

Date of birth
(actual or estimated) _____

Breed _____   Sex _____

Colour/description _____

_____

(photograph or portrait)

Feeding notes _____

_____

_____

_____

_____

_____

_____

_____

Medical record _____

_____

_____

_____

_____

_____

_____

_____

Breeding record (if applicable)
or
date of neutering operation _____

_____

_____

_____

_____

_____

_____

_____

Veterinary surgeon's name _____

Practice address _____

_____

Surgery hours _____

_____

Tel. no. _____

Vaccination at age 10-12 weeks

	date	Age of kitten	Veterinary surgeon
feline enteritis			
feline influenza			

Booster injections, as recommended by veterinary surgeon: dates: _____

Index